MW00529068

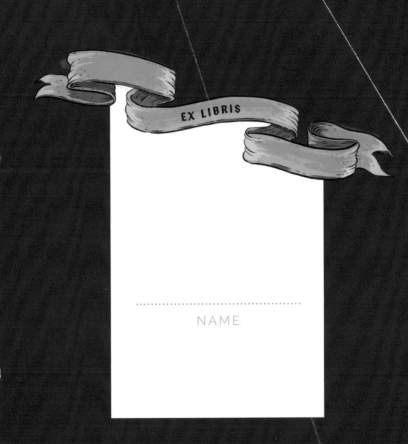

EX LIBRIS

....

NAME

ACROSTIC THEOLOGY FOR KIDS SERIES

A RHYMING CHRISTOLOGY FOR KIDS

THE
ACROSTIC
OF
JESUS

JONATHAN GIBSON & TIMOTHY BRINDLE

ILLUSTRATED BY
C. S. FRITZ

New
Growth
Press

New Growth Press, Greensboro, NC 27404
Text Copyright © 2022 by Jonathan Gibson and Timothy Brindle
Illustration Copyright © 2022 by C. S. Fritz

Cover/Interior Design and Typesetting: Trish Mahoney, themahoney.com
Cover/Interior illustrations: C. S. Fritz
Art typeset in Cinder by Fort Foundry

ISBN: 978-1-64507-204-1
Library of Congress Control Number: 2021937301

Printed in Canada

29 28 27 26 25 24 23 22   1 2 3 4 5

The Acrostic Theology for Kids Series

"And these words that I command you today shall be on your heart. You shall teach them diligently to your children, and shall talk of them when you sit in your house, and when you walk by the way, and when you lie down, and when you rise." Deuteronomy 6:6–7

The inspiration behind these acrostic books comes from John Calvin, the Genevan Reformer. In 1542, Calvin simplified his Catechism for the Genevan Church (1537) so that children could better understand and memorize the essential truths of the Christian Faith. It was entitled *The French ABCs*.

These acrostic books are not strictly catechetical (questions and answers), but they are written in that same tradition of instruction. As such, they are a means of planting the good seed of God's Word into the hearts of children, so that they might grow in the grace and knowledge of the Lord Jesus. We hope the new element of an acrostic poem set to rhyme may help the truths about God (theology), Jesus (Christology), salvation (soteriology), and Scripture (Biblical theology) to stick a little bit better. The books may be read in one sitting (either by parent/teacher or child) or they may be used for family devotions, taking one letter per day for families to meditate on, with some accompanying Bible verses.

We are praying that this series will be used by the Spirit to allow children and parents to grow in the knowledge of God and thus to love and trust him more. Enjoy!

Jonny Gibson and Timothy Brindle

See back of book for more information about how to use this book with children. Use the QR code to hear Timothy Brindle read aloud *The Acrostic of Jesus* in rap style. To purchase *The Acrostic of Jesus* music album, visit www.timothybrindleministries.com.

Dedication

For our nephews and nieces:

Archie, Ella, Samuel, and Lily; Kye, Izak, and Cruz; and Ella

Maarley, Leghaand, Taalib, Maaliq, Journie, Destiny, Achava, Yehoyakim; Daniel and John Cooper

Though you have not seen Jesus,
may you love him all your days
1 Peter 1:8a

Prologue

Let's read the *Acrostic of Jesus together*
To help you to love him, so *he is your treasure.*
We'll read it, rap it, or sing it—*it's fun!*
Till Jesus comes back and his kingdom *has come.*

An acrostic poem uses the *alphabet*
To teach you about Christ, so you will *not forget.*
God does this in Scripture, like Psalm *One Nineteen;*
In Lamentations, he has a *fun rhyme scheme.*
So, from now on, we'll use the *first letter*
To help you remember and to *learn better.*
He's the Alpha and Omega, from *A to Z;*
We pray you see from this book, "Jesus *came for me!"*

Each page will have a name, *attribute, or a title*
Of Jesus Christ *that is rooted in the Bible.*
He says, "In all your ways, *acknowledge me"*—
Kids, you're not too young to learn *Christology!*
What is Christology? It's the *study of Jesus,*
Of his person and work, and how he *does what he pleases.*
Not just to know about him *more in our brains,*
But to know him as the Lord of *glory who reigns.*

So . . .

Let's read the *Acrostic of Jesus together*
To help you to love him, so *he is your treasure.*
We'll read it, rap it, or *sing it—it's fun!*
Till Jesus comes back and his kingdom *has come.*

ABLE

ABLE to rescue, Jesus has the *power to save;*

He can redeem sinners, who are *bound as a slave.*

Jesus helps children, who don't know *how to behave;*

He can even raise the dead, who are *down in the grave!*

....

Hebrews 7:25 Consequently, **he is able to save to the uttermost** those who draw near to God through him, since he always lives to make intercession for them.

Bread of Life

BREAD OF LIFE from heaven, that's what *Jesus gives;*
He gives us himself—we live because *Jesus lives.*
Yes, he is bread for our souls, not just for our *tummies;*
Without Jesus, we're dead like Egyptian *mummies.*

....

John 6:51 "I am the living bread that came down from heaven. If anyone eats of this bread, he will live forever. And the bread that I will give for the life of the world is my flesh."

CHRIST

CHRIST means Messiah—Jesus is *God's Anointed One;*

The Spirit was poured upon him as *God's Appointed Son.*

By Christ our King, we're *saved from our sins;*

Jesus sits on David's throne; he *reigns and he wins!*

....

1 Timothy 1:15 The saying is trustworthy and deserving of full acceptance, that **Christ Jesus came into the world to save sinners,** of whom I am the foremost.

Door

DOOR of the sheepfold—*Jesus is the way in,*
For all the wanderin' *sheep who were strayin'.*
As the door to the kingdom, he's the only *entrance;*
Anyone can go in, through faith and *repentance.*

....

John 10:9 "I am the door. If anyone enters by me, he will be saved and will go in and out and find pasture."

Everlasting

EVERLASTING means Jesus has no beginning or *end;*
He was always with the Father, before the plan to *descend.*
God's Son needed nothing *before he came to earth;*
He was happy in heaven *before his famous birth!*

....

John 1:1–2 In the beginning was the Word, and the Word was with God, and the Word was God. **He was in the beginning with God.**

FAITHFUL

FAITHFUL, because Jesus keeps every *promise;*

He can't lie—we don't have to doubt like *Thomas.*

His resurrection proves every promise is *true,*

Especially the one to be the God of me and *you.*

---

2 Timothy 2:13 "If we are faithless, **he remains faithful**"—for he cannot deny himself.

God

GOD—"fully divine"—that is who *Jesus is;*

He knows all things and he always *sees us, kids.*

But he's also "fully human," since born of a *virgin;*

So Jesus is the God-Man—two natures in one *person.*

....

Colossians 1:19 For in him all the fullness of God was pleased to dwell.

Colossians 2:9 For in him the whole fullness of deity dwells [in] bodily [form].

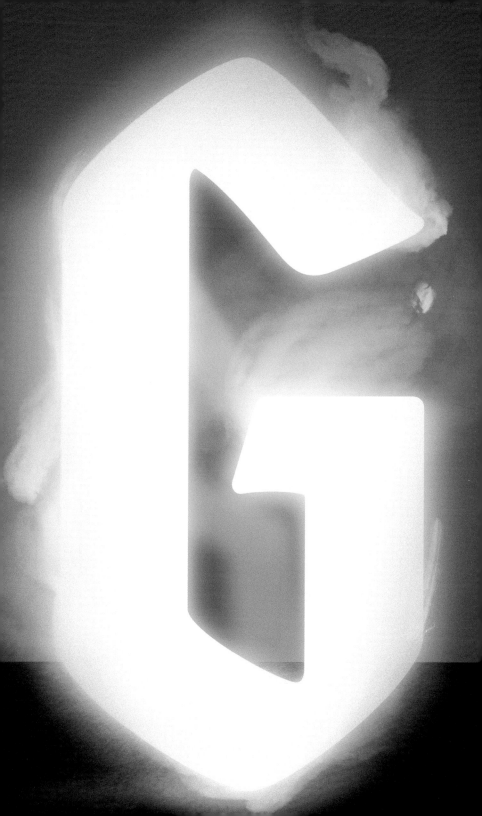

Humble

HUMBLE means selfless, so Jesus didn't *serve himself;*

He laid aside his glory and his *eternal wealth.*

Although he is God—*"Holy, Holy, Holy!"*—

To make us his own, he made himself *lowly.*

Although he is holy, and *hates all our sin,*

Jesus lowered himself to *make us his kin.*

He humbled himself, even to *death on a tree;*

Jesus died for sinners who are *wretched like me.*

....

Philippians 2:6–8 Though he [Jesus] was in the form of God, [he] did not count equality with God a thing to be grasped, but emptied himself, by taking the form of a servant, being born in the likeness of men. And being found in human form, **he humbled himself by becoming obedient to the point of death, even death on a cross.**

Immanuel

IMMANUEL in Hebrew means *"God with us";*

He'll be with us forever; we haven't *got to fuss.*

If you abide in him, then he'll *abide in you;*

He'll give his Holy Spirit to dwell *inside you, too.*

Matthew 1:23 "Behold, the virgin shall conceive and bear a son, and they shall call his name **Immanuel**" (which means, **God with us**).

"Jesus"

"JESUS" means that he will save us from our *nasty sin;*

Over its guilt and its power, he *has to win.*

So when you hear "Jesus," think "God's *salvation";*

Dying and rising, he makes us a new *creation.*

....

Matthew 1:21 "She will bear a son, and you shall call his name Jesus, for he will save his people from their sins."

2 Corinthians 5:17 Therefore, if anyone is in Christ, he is a new creation. The old has passed away; behold, the new has come.

King

KING Jesus, he is the Ruler of God's *Kingdom;*

When God made Adam, he made him king with *dominion.*

But since Adam sinned, death and Satan reigned *instead,*

Until God sent Jesus to crush the Serpent's *head.*

. . . .

Genesis 3:15 "I will put enmity between you and the woman, and between your offspring and her offspring; **he shall crush your head,** although you shall crush his heel." (AT)

1 Corinthians 15:25–26 For he must reign until he has put all his enemies under his feet. **The last enemy to be destroyed is death.**

LIGHT

LIGHT of the World, because Jesus shines in the *darkness*;

To overcome our sin, he broke through our *hardness*.

He gives us new eyes; no longer *blinded by evil;*

Now the Light of the World still *shines through his people!*

. . . .

John 8:12 Again Jesus spoke to them, saying, "**I am the light of the world**. Whoever follows me will not walk in darkness, but will have the **light of life**."

Mediator

MEDIATOR—he stands between us and *our Maker*,

Because against God, you and me have been a *traitor*.

So Jesus ransomed us when he paid for our *sin*;

God isn't mad at us—now he welcomes us *in*.

. . . .

1 Timothy 2:5–6 For there is one God, and there is one mediator between God and men, the man Christ Jesus, who gave himself as a ransom for all, which is the testimony given at the proper time.

Luke 6:13–16 And when day came, he called his disciples and chose from them twelve . . . : Simon, whom he called Peter, and Andrew his brother . . . and Judas Iscariot, who became a traitor.

No Other Name

NO OTHER NAME under heaven has been *provided,*

To bring God and sinners together, *undivided.*

Jesus's blood paid for what we couldn't *afford,*

So God gave him the greatest Name, which is *Lord!*

....

Acts 4:12 "And there is salvation in no one else, **for there is no other name under heaven given among men by which we must be saved.**"

OBEDIENT

OBEDIENT to the law—Jesus never *sinned at all;*

But you and I, every single day, we *slip and fall.*

Like when we're selfish and won't share our *donut;*

Jesus lived perfectly as a kid and a *grown-up.*

Every day of his life he obeyed his Father and *mother,*

But for rebel kids he gave his life as our *brother.*

When we believe in him, God sees us with his *perfection;*

We're saved as much by his life, as by his death and *resurrection.*

....

Romans 5:19 For as by the one man's disobedience the many were made sinners, so by the one man's obedience the many will be made righteous.

PROPHET AND PRIEST

PROPHET and PRIEST—Christ fulfills both *offices;*

He gives you God's Word—that's what a *prophet is.*

As priest, he became the Lamb led to the *slaughter,*

And now he intercedes for you, his son or his *daughter.*

. . . .

Acts 3:22 "Moses said, 'The Lord God will raise up for you a prophet like me from your brothers. You shall listen to him in whatever he tells you.'"

Hebrews 7:21 "The Lord has sworn and will not change his mind, 'You are a priest forever.'"

Quick

QUICK to forgive, Jesus is very *swift to bless,*

So every time we sin, we can *quickly confess.*

Now let's be ready to repent and *seek his forgiveness;*

He'll remove our sins, and one day, *diseases and sickness.*

....

Mark 2:5 And when Jesus saw their faith, he said to the paralytic, "**Son, your sins are forgiven.**"

Mark 2:10–12 "But that you may know that the Son of Man has authority on earth to forgive sins"— he said to the paralytic—"I say to you, rise, pick up your bed, and go home." **And he rose and immediately picked up his bed and went out before them all.**

Resurrection

RESURRECTION, because Jesus gives *life to the dead;*

Before he was risen, he gave his *life in our stead.*

See, all of us will die, returning *back to the dust;*

But he'll raise us like Lazarus—we just *have to trust.*

Without sin, he is righteous, born of a *virgin;*

By his resurrection, our salvation is *certain.*

Now he is risen, ruling, and *reigning;*

Soon he'll be returning, to begin the final *raising!*

. . . .

John 11:25–26 Jesus said to her, "**I am the resurrection and the life.** Whoever believes in me, though he die, yet shall he live, and everyone who lives and believes in me shall never die. Do you believe this?"

Roman 4:24–25 It will be counted to us who believe in him who raised from the dead Jesus our Lord, **who was delivered up for our trespasses and raised for our justification.**

SHEPHERD

SHEPHERD of the flock, he is the *Shepherd who's good;*

Jesus died for his sheep when he *bled on the wood.*

From the nails of the cross, he has *holes in his hands;*

With those same hands, the Savior's *holding his lambs.*

....

Psalm 23:4 Even though I walk through the valley of the shadow of death, I will fear no evil, for you are with me; **your rod and your staff, they comfort me.**

John 10:11 "I am the good shepherd. The good shepherd lays down his life for the sheep."

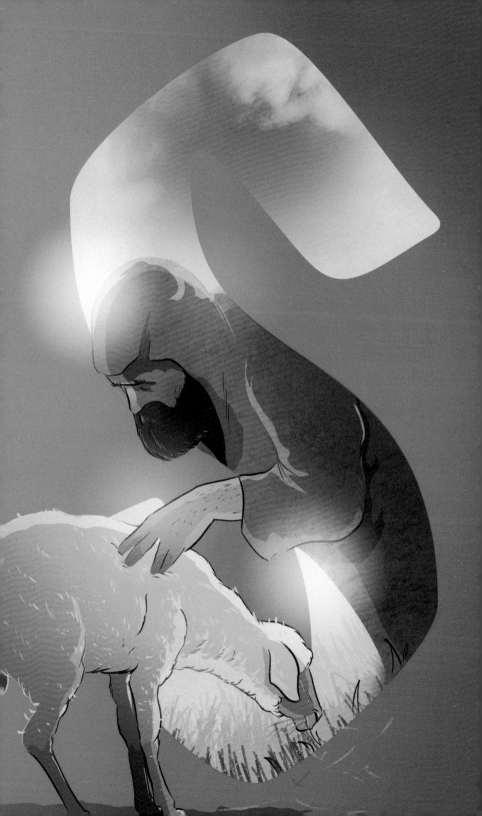

TENDER

TENDER and compassionate, Jesus *feels all our pain;*

Seen in cleansing the leper and *healing the lame.*

He mourns with us, when we cry and *weep from our loss;*

The Man of Sorrows carried our *griefs to the cross.*

....

Mark 1:41 Moved with compassion, Jesus stretched out his hand and touched him, and said to him, "I am willing; be cleansed." (AT)

John 11:35 Jesus wept.

Hebrews 4:15 For we do not have a high priest who is unable to sympathize with our weaknesses, but one who in every respect has been tempted as we are, yet without sin.

Unchangeable

UNCHANGEABLE—change is impossible for God to *do;*

He is incapable of shifting in his love for *you.*

Will God's faithfulness to you ever change? No! No! *Never!*

Jesus is the same yesterday, today, and *forever!*

....

Hebrews 13:8 Jesus Christ is the same yesterday and today and forever.

VINE

VINE—the True Vine—that's a picture of *Jesus;*

So we are the branches, that's how he *sees us.*

If we turn away from him, then we'll *fall and die;*

But if we stay connected, our fruit will *multiply.*

. . . .

John 15:5 "I am the vine; you are the branches. Whoever abides in me and I in him, he it is that bears much fruit, for apart from me you can do nothing."

WATER

WATER for our souls, which we need to stay *a-livin';*

Christ gives the Water that flowed from his side *a-riven.*

If we drink his Living Water, our hearts will never *thirst;*

So don't go after idols, children—put Jesus *first!*

. . . .

John 4:13–14 Jesus said to her, "Everyone who drinks of this water will be thirsty again, but whoever drinks of the water that I will give him will never be thirsty again. **The water that I will give him will become in him a spring of water welling up to eternal life.**"

EXALTED

EXALTED above, Jesus is super-*duper high!*

When he rose from the dead, he went up *through the sky.*

Jesus entered into heaven, then he took his *seat*

At the Father's right hand, with all things under his *feet.*

....

Philippians 2:9–11 Therefore God has highly exalted him and bestowed on him the name that is above every name, so that at the name of Jesus every knee should bow, in heaven and on earth and under the earth, and every tongue confess that Jesus Christ is Lord, to the glory of God the Father.

Acts 2:32–33 "This Jesus God raised up, and of that we all are witnesses. Being therefore exalted at the right hand of God, and having received from the Father the promise of the Holy Spirit, he has poured out this that you yourselves are seeing and hearing."

Yahweh

YAHWEH—this is God's covenant name in *Hebrew;*

Moses said to Israel, "I AM sent me *to you."*

So when Jesus came to earth and said, *"I AM,"*

He was saying, "God's the Passover *Lamb."*

....

Exodus 3:14–15 God said to Moses, "I AM WHO I AM." And he said, "Say this to the people of Israel: 'I AM has sent me to you.'" God also said to Moses, "Say this to the people of Israel: 'The LORD, the God of your fathers, the God of Abraham, the God of Isaac, and the God of Jacob, has sent me to you.' This is my name forever, and thus I am to be remembered throughout all generations."

1 Corinthians 5:7 For Christ, our Passover lamb, has been sacrificed.

Zealous

ZEALOUS—as Psalm 69 and John 2 *tell us*,

that for God's glory, Jesus is always *jealous.*

He hates it when we don't give God all the *praise;*

By his Holy Spirit, he sets our souls *ablaze.*

....

Psalm 69:9 For zeal for your house has consumed me, and the reproaches of those who reproach you have fallen on me.

John 2:16–17 And he told those who sold the pigeons, "Take these things away; do not make my Father's house a house of trade." His disciples remembered that it was written, "**Zeal for your house will consume me.**"

Closing Refrain

Now we've read the Acrostic of *Jesus together,*

Let's pray: "Father, please make *Jesus our treasure.*

We thank you for who he is and *what he has done.*

Father in heaven, help us *trust in your Son."*

RHYME YOUR ACROSTIC

Since the beginning of time, human beings have been using acrostics
and rhyme as a teaching tool. Putting ideas into an acrostic rhyme
helps children to learn things in a more memorable way than
simple rote learning. God, the author of all language, knows this.
The Bible is full of poetry. It contains acrostic poems that begin
lines with each letter of the Hebrew alphabet (e.g., Psalm 119 and
the book of Lamentations); it also contains poems that emphasize
rhyme in Hebrew (e.g., Psalms 1 and 2). These poetic features make
the content of God's Word easier to remember. Acrostic poems
are straightforward, covering each letter of the alphabet, A–Z. The
Acrostic Theology for Kids series is written as a rap. Children might
be more familiar with this style of rhyme than their parents. If you
need some help reading it, there is a QR code at the end of the book
that you can scan to hear Timothy Brindle read *The Acrostic of Jesus*
 in a rap style.

Basic Truths to Memorize with Children

THE LORD'S PRAYER

OUR FATHER in heaven,
hallowed be your name,
your kingdom come,
your will be done,
on earth as it is in heaven.
Give us this day our daily bread;
And forgive us our debts,
as we forgive our debtors.
And lead us not into temptation
but deliver us from evil.
For yours is the kingdom, and the power,
and the glory, forever. Amen.

THE TEN COMMANDMENTS

AND GOD spoke all these words, saying, I am the LORD your God, who brought you out of the land of Egypt, out of the house of slavery.

1. You shall have no other gods before me.

2. You shall not make for yourself a carved image, or any likeness of anything that is in heaven above, or that is in the earth beneath, or that is in the water under the earth.

3. You shall not take the name of the LORD your God in vain, for the LORD will not hold him guiltless who takes his name in vain.

4. Remember the Sabbath day, to keep it holy. Six days you shall labor, and do all your work, but the seventh day is a Sabbath to the LORD your God.

5. Honor your father and your mother, that your days may be long in the land that the LORD your God is giving you.

6. You shall not murder.

7. You shall not commit adultery.

8. You shall not steal.

9. You shall not bear false witness against your neighbor.

10. You shall not covet your neighbor's house; you shall not covet your neighbor's wife, or his male servant, or his female servant, or his ox, or his donkey, or anything that is your neighbor's.

THE APOSTLES' CREED

I BELIEVE in God, the Father Almighty,
    Maker of heaven and earth.

I believe in Jesus Christ, his only-begotten Son, our Lord;
    who was conceived by the Holy Spirit,
    born of the Virgin Mary;
    suffered under Pontius Pilate;
    was crucified, dead, and buried;
    he descended into hell;
    the third day he rose again from the dead;
    he ascended into heaven,
    and sits at the right hand of God the Father Almighty;
    from there he shall come to judge the living and the dead.

I believe in the Holy Spirit;
    the holy catholic Church;
    the communion of saints;
    the forgiveness of sins;
    the resurrection of the body;
    and the life everlasting. Amen.

....

Scan this QR code to hear Timothy Brindle read *The Acrostic of Jesus* in a rap style. To purchase *The Acrostic of Jesus* music album, visit www.timothybrindleministries.com.